Anatolius and Minor Writers

Anatolius and Minor Writers

Anatolius and Minor Writers

© Lighthouse Publishing 2024

Written by: Anatolius (230 – 270-280AD)
Translated by: Rev. S. D. F. Salmond, M.A. (1838 – 20 April 1905)
Updated into Modern U.S English: A.M. Overett (b.1960)

All rights reserved. Without limiting the rights under copyright reserved above, no part of this publication may be reproduced,stored in a retrieval system, or transmitted, in any form or by any means (electronic, mechanical, photocopying, recording or otherwise), without the prior written permission of the copyright owner of this book.

Published by
Lighthouse Publishing
SAN 257-4330
228 Freedom Parkway
Hoschton, GA 30548
United States of America

www.lighthousechristianpublishing.com

Introductory Notice
to
Anatolius and Minor Writers.

Instead of reprinting a disjointed mass of "Fragments," I have thought it desirable to present them in a group, illustrative of the Alexandrian school. I give to Anatolius the deserved place of prominence, marking him as the meet successor of Africanus in ability if not in the nature of his pursuits. His writing and the testimony of Eusebius prove him to have been a star of no inferior magnitude, even in the brilliant constellation of faith and genius of which he is part.

These minor writers I have arranged, not with exclusive reference to minute chronology,
but with some respect to their material, as follows:—

I. Anatolius, a.d. 270.
II. Alexander of Cappadocia, a.d. 250.
III. Theognostus, a.d. 265.
IV. Pierius, a.d. 300.
V. Theonas, a.d. 300.
VI. Phileas, a.d. 307.
VII. Pamphilus, a.d. 309.

Anatolius and Minor Writers.

Anatolius of Alexandria.

Translator's Biographical Notice.

[a.d. 230–270–280.] From Jerome we learn that Anatolius flourished in the reign of Probus and Carus, that he was a native of Alexandria, and that he became bishop of Laodicea. Eusebius gives a somewhat lengthened account of him, and speaks of him in terms of the strongest laudation, as one surpassing all the men of his time in learning and science. He tells us that he attained the highest eminence in arithmetic, geometry, and astronomy, besides being a great proficient also in dialectics, physics, and rhetoric. His reputation was so great among the Alexandrians that they are said to have requested him to open a school for teaching the Aristotelian philosophy in their city. He did great service to his fellow-citizens in Alexandria on their being besieged by the Romans in a.d. 262, and was the means of saving the lives of numbers of them. After this he is said to have passed into Syria, where Theotecnus, the bishop of Cæsareia, ordained him, destining him to be his own successor in the bishopric. After this, however, having occasion to travel to Antioch to attend the synod convened to deal with the case of Paul of Samosata, as he passed through the city of Laodicea, he was detained by the people and made bishop of the place, in succession to Eusebius. This must have been about the year 270 a.d. How long he held that dignity, however, we do not know. Eusebius tells us that he did not write many books, but yet enough to show us at once his eloquence and his erudition. Among these was a treatise on the *Chronology of Easter*; of which a considerable extract is preserved in Eusebius. The book itself exists now only in a Latin version, which is generally ascribed to Rufinus, and which was published by Ægidius Bucherius in his *Doctrina Temporum*, which was issued at Antwerp in 1634. Another work of his was the *Institutes of Arithmetic*, of which we have some fragments in the θεολογούμενα τῆς ἀριθμητικῆς, which was published in Paris in 1543. Some small fragments of his mathematical works, which have also come down to us, were published by Fabricius in his *Bibliotheca Græca*, iii. p. 462.

The Paschal Canon of Anatolius of Alexandria.

I.

As we are about to speak on the subject of the order of the times and alternations of the world, we shall first dispose of the positions of diverse calculators; who, by reckoning only by the course of the moon, and leaving out of account the ascent and descent of the sun, with the addition of certain problems, have constructed diverse periods, self-contradictory, and such as are never found in the reckoning of a true computation; since it is certain that no mode of computation is to be approved, in which these two measures are not found together. For even in the ancient exemplars, that is, in the books of the Hebrews and Greeks, we find not only the course of the moon, but also that of the sun, and, indeed, not simply its course in the general, but even the separate and minutest moments of its hours all calculated, as we shall show at the proper time, when the matter in hand demands it. Of these Hippolytus made up a period of sixteen years with certain unknown courses of the moon. Others have reckoned by a period of twenty-five years, others by thirty, and some by eighty-four years, without, however, teaching thereby an exact method of calculating Easter. But our predecessors, men most learned in the books of the Hebrews and Greeks,—I mean Isidore and Jerome and Clement,— although they have noted similar beginnings for the months just as they differ also in language, have, nevertheless, come harmoniously to one and the same most exact reckoning of Easter, day and month and season meeting in accord with the highest honor for the Lord's resurrection. But Origen also, the most erudite of all, and the acutest in making calculations,—a man, too, to whom the epithet χαλκευτής is given,—has published in a very elegant manner a little book on Easter. And in this book, while declaring, with respect to the day of Easter, that attention must be given not only to the course of the moon and the transit of the equinox, but also to the passage (*transcensum*) of the sun, which removes every foul ambush and offence of all darkness, and brings on the advent of light and the power and inspiration of the elements of the whole world, he speaks thus: In the (matter of the) day of Easter, he remarks, I do not say that it is to be observed that the Lord's day should be found, and the seven days of the moon which are to elapse, but that the sun should pass that division, to wit, between light and darkness, constituted in an equality by the dispensation of the Lord at the beginning of the world; and that, from one hour to two hours, from two to three, from three to four, from four to five, from five to six hours, while the light is increasing in the ascent of the sun, the darkness should decrease....and the addition of the twentieth number being completed, twelve parts should be supplied in one and the same day. But if I should have attempted to add any little drop of mine after the exuberant streams of the eloquence and science of some, what else should there be to believe but that it should be ascribed by all to ostentation, and, to speak more truly, to madness, did not the assistance of your promised prayers animate us for a little? For we believe that nothing is impossible to your power of prayer, and to your faith. Strengthened, therefore, by this confidence, we shall set bashfulness aside, and shall enter this most deep and unforeseen sea of the obscurest calculation, in which swelling questions and problems surge around us on all sides.

II.

There is, then, in the first year, the new moon of the first month, which is the beginning of every cycle of nineteen years, on the six and twentieth day of the month called by the Egyptians Phamenoth. But, according to the months of the Macedonians, it is on the two-and-twentieth day of Dystrus. And, as the Romans would say, it is on the eleventh day before the Kalends of April. Now the sun is found on the said six-and-twentieth day of Phamenoth, not only as having mounted to the first segment, but as already passing the fourth day in it. And this segment they are accustomed to call the first dodecatemorion (twelfth part), and the equinox, and the beginning of months, and the head of the cycle, and the starting-point of the course of the planets. And the segment before this they call the last of the months, and the twelfth segment, and the last dodecatemorion, and the end of the circuit of the planets. And for this reason, also, we maintain that those who place the first month in it, and who determine the fourteenth day of the Paschal season by it, make no trivial or common blunder.

III.

Nor is this an opinion confined to ourselves alone. For it was also known to the Jews of old and before Christ, and it was most carefully observed by them. And this may be learned from what Philo, and Josephus, and Musæus have written; and not only from these, but indeed from others still more ancient, namely, the two Agathobuli, who were surnamed the Masters, and the eminent Aristobulus, who was one of the Seventy who translated the sacred and holy Scriptures of the Hebrews for Ptolemy Philadelphus and his father, and dedicated his exegetical books on the law of Moses to the same kings. These writers, in solving some questions which are raised with respect to Exodus, say that all alike ought to sacrifice the Passover after the vernal equinox in the middle of the first month. And that is found to be when the sun passes through the first segment of the solar, or, as some among them have named it, the zodiacal circle.

IV.

But this Aristobulus also adds, that for the feast of the Passover it was necessary not only that the sun should pass the equinoctial segment, but the moon also. For as there are two equinoctial segments, the vernal and the autumnal, and these diametrically opposite to each other, and since the day of the Passover is fixed for the fourteenth day of the month, in the evening, the moon will have the position diametrically opposite the sun; as is to be seen in full moons. And the sun will thus be in the segment of the vernal equinox, and the moon necessarily will be at the autumnal equinox.

V.

I am aware that very many other matters were discussed by them, some of them with considerable probability, and others of them as matters of the clearest demonstration, by which they endeavor to prove that the festival of the Passover and unleavened bread ought by all means to be kept after the equinox. But I shall pass on without demanding such copious demonstrations (on subjects) from which the veil of the Mosaic law has been removed; for now it remains for us with unveiled face to behold ever as in a glass Christ Himself and the doctrines and sufferings of Christ. But that the first month among the Hebrews is about the equinox, is clearly shown also by what is taught in the book of Enoch.

VI.

And, therefore, in this concurrence of the sun and moon, the Paschal festival is not to be celebrated, because as long as they are found in this course the power of darkness is not overcome; and as long as equality between light and darkness endures, and is not diminished by the light, it is shown that the Paschal festival is not to be celebrated. Accordingly, it is enjoined that that festival be kept after the equinox, because the moon of the fourteenth, if before the equinox or at the equinox, does not fill the whole night. But after the equinox, the moon of the fourteenth, with one day being added because of the passing of the equinox, although it does not extend to the true light, that is, the rising of the sun and the beginning of day, will nevertheless leave no darkness behind it. And, in accordance with this, Moses is charged by the Lord to keep seven days of unleavened bread for the celebration of the Passover, that in them no power of darkness should be found to surpass the light. And although the outset of four nights begins to be dark, that is, the 17th and 18th and 19th and 20th, yet the moon of the 20th, which rises before that, does not permit the darkness to extend on even to midnight.

VII.

To us, however, with whom it is impossible for all these things to come aptly at one and the same time, namely, the moon's fourteenth, and the Lord's day, and the passing of the equinox, and whom the obligation of the Lord's resurrection binds to keep the Paschal festival on the Lord's day, it is granted that we may extend the beginning of our celebration even to the moon's twentieth. For although the moon of the 20th does not fill the whole night, yet, rising as it does in the second watch, it illumines the greater part of the night. Certainly if the rising of the moon should be delayed on to the end of two watches, that is to say, to midnight, the light would not then exceed the darkness, but the darkness the light. But it is clear that in the Paschal feast it is not possible that any part of the darkness should surpass the light; for the festival of the Lord's resurrection is *one of* light, and there is no fellowship between light and darkness. And if the moon should rise in the third watch, it is clear that the 22d or 23d of the moon would then be reached, in which it is not possible that there can be a true celebration of Easter. For those who determine that the festival may be kept at this age of the moon, are not only unable to make that good by the authority of Scripture, but turn also into the crime of sacrilege and contumacy, and incur the peril of their souls; inasmuch as they affirm that the true light may be celebrated along with something of that power of darkness which dominates all.

VIII.

Accordingly, it is not the case, as certain calculators of Gaul allege, that this assertion is opposed by that passage in Exodus, where we read: "In the first month, on the fourteenth day of the first month, at even, ye shall eat unleavened bread until the one-and twentieth day of the month at even. Seven days shall there be no leaven found in your houses." From this they maintain that it is quite permissible to celebrate the Passover on the twenty-first day of the moon; understanding that if the twenty-second day were added, there would be found eight days of unleavened bread. A thing which cannot be found with any probability, indeed, in the Old Testament, as the Lord, through Moses, gives this charge: "Seven days ye shall eat unleavened bread." Unless perchance the fourteenth day is not reckoned by them among the days of unleavened bread with the celebration of the feast; which, however, is contrary to the Word of the Gospel which says: "Moreover, on the first day of unleavened bread, the disciples came to Jesus." And there is no doubt as to its being the fourteenth day on which the disciples asked the Lord, in accordance with the custom established for them of old, "Where wilt Thou that we prepare for Thee to eat the Passover?" But they who are deceived with this error maintain this addition, because they do not know that the 13th and 14th, the 14th and 15th, the 15th and 16th, the 16th and 17th, the 17th and 18th, the 18th and 19th, the 19th and 20th, the 20th and 21st days of the moon are each found, as may be most surely proved, within a single day. For every day in the reckoning of the moon does not end in the evening as the same day in respect of number, as it is at its beginning in the morning. For the day which in the morning, that is up to the sixth hour and half, is numbered the 13th day of the month, is found at even to be the 14th. Wherefore, also, the Passover is enjoined to be extended on to the 21st day at even; which day, without doubt, in the morning, that is, up to that term of hours which we have mentioned, was reckoned the 20th. Calculate, then, from the end of the 13th1177 day of the moon, which marks the beginning of the 14th, on to the end of the 20th, at which the 21st day also begins, and you will have only seven days of unleavened bread, in which, by the guidance of the Lord, it has been determined before that the most true feast of the Passover ought to be celebrated.

IX.

But what wonder is it that they should have erred in the matter of the 21st day of the moon who have added three days before the equinox, in which they hold that the Passover may be celebrated? An assertion which certainly must be considered altogether absurd, since, by the best-known historiographers of the Jews, and by the Seventy Elders, it has been clearly determined that the Paschal festival cannot be celebrated at the equinox.

X.

But nothing was difficult to them with whom it was lawful to celebrate the Passover on any day when the fourteenth of the moon happened after the equinox. Following their example up to the present time all the bishops of Asia—as themselves also receiving the rule from an unimpeachable authority, to wit, the evangelist John, who leant on the Lord's breast, and drank in instructions spiritual without doubt—were in the way of celebrating the Paschal feast, without question, every year, whenever the fourteenth day of the moon had come, and the lamb was sacrificed by the Jews after the equinox was past; not acquiescing, so far as regards this matter, with the authority of some, namely, the successors of Peter and Paul, who have taught all the churches in which they sowed the spiritual seeds of the Gospel, that the solemn festival of the resurrection of the Lord can be celebrated only on the Lord's day. Whence, also, a certain contention broke out between the successors of these, namely, Victor, at that time bishop of the city of Rome, and Polycrates, who then appeared to hold the primacy among the bishops of Asia. And this contention was adjusted most rightfully by Irenæus, at that time president of a part of Gaul, so that both parties kept by their own order, and did not decline from the original custom of antiquity. The one party, indeed, kept the Paschal day on the fourteenth day of the first month, according to the Gospel, as they thought, adding nothing of an extraneous kind, but keeping through all things the rule of faith. And the other party, passing the day of the Lord's Passion as one replete with sadness and grief, hold that it should not be lawful to celebrate the Lord's mystery of the Passover at any other time but on the Lord's day, on which the resurrection of the Lord from death took place, and on which rose also for us the cause of everlasting joy. For it is one thing to act in accordance with the precept given by the apostle, yea, by the Lord Himself, and be sad with the sad, and suffer with him that suffers by the cross, His own word being: "My soul is exceeding sorrowful, even unto death;" and it is another thing to rejoice with the victor as he triumphs over an ancient enemy, and exults with the highest triumph over a conquered adversary, as He Himself also says: "Rejoice with Me; for I have found the sheep which I had lost."

XI.

Moreover, the allegation which they sometimes make against us, that if we pass the moon's fourteenth we cannot celebrate the beginning of the Paschal feast in light, neither moves nor disturbs us. For, although they lay it down as a thing unlawful, that the beginning of the Paschal festival should be extended so far as to the moon's twentieth; yet they cannot deny that it ought to be extended to the sixteenth and seventeenth, which coincide with the day on which the Lord rose from the dead. But we decide that it is better that it should be extended even on to the twentieth day, on account of the Lord's day, than that we should anticipate the Lord's day on account of the fourteenth day; for on the Lord's day was it that light was shown to us in the beginning, and now also in the end, the comforts of all present and the tokens of all future blessings. For the Lord ascribes no less praise to the twentieth day than to the fourteenth. For in the book of Leviticus the injunction is expressed thus: "In the first month, on the fourteenth day of this month, at even, is the Lord's Passover. And on the fifteenth day of this month is the feast of unleavened bread unto the Lord. Seven days ye shall eat unleavened bread. The first day shall be to you one most diligently attended and holy. Ye shall do no servile work thereon. And the seventh day shall be to you more diligently attended and holier; ye shall do no servile work thereon." And hence we maintain that those have contracted no guilt before the tribunal of Christ, who have held that the beginning of the Paschal festival ought to be extended to this day. And this, too, the most especially, as we are pressed by three difficulties, namely, that we should keep the solemn festival of the Passover on the Lord's day, and after the equinox, and yet not beyond the limit of the moon's twentieth day.

XII.

But this again is held by other wise and most acute men to be an impossibility, because within that narrow and most contracted limit of a cycle of nineteen years, a thoroughly genuine Paschal time, that is to say, one held on the Lord's day and yet after the equinox, cannot occur. But, in order that we may set in a clearer light the difficulty which causes their incredulity, we shall set down, along with the courses of the moon, that cycle of years which we have mentioned; the days being computed before in which the year rolls on in its alternating courses, by Kalends and Ides and Nones, and by the sun's ascent and descent.

XIII.

The moon's age set forth in the Julian calendar.

January, on the Kalends, one day, the moon's first (day); on the Nones, the 5th day, the moon's 5th; on the Ides, the 13th day, the moon's 13th. On the day before the Kalends of February, the 31st day, the moon's 1st; on the Kalends of February, the 32d day, the moon's 2d; on the Nones, the 36th day, the moon's 6th; on the Ides, the 44th day, the moon's 14th. On the day before the Kalends of March, the 59th day, the moon's 29th; on the Kalends of

March, the 60th day, the moon's 1st; on the Nones, the 66th day, the moon's 7th; on the Ides, the 74th day, the moon's 15th. On the day before the Kalends of April, the 90th day, the moon's 2d; on the Kalends of April, the 91st day, the moon's 3d; on the Nones, the 95th day, the moon's 7th; on the Ides, the 103d day, the moon's 15th. On the day before the Kalends of May, the 120th day, the moon's 3d; on the Kalends of May, the 121st day, the moon's 4th; on the Nones, the 127th day, the moon's 10th; on the Ides, the 135th day, the moon's 18th. On the day before the Kalends of June, the 151st day, the moon's 3d; on the Kalends of June, the 152d day, the moon's 5th; on the Nones, the 153d day, the moon's 9th; on the Ides, the 164th day, the moon's 17th. On the day before the Kalends of July, the 181st day, the moon's 5th; on the Kalends of July, the 182d day, the moon's 6th; on the Nones, the 188th day, the moon's 12th; on the Ides, the 196th day, the moon's 20th. On the day before the Kalends of August, the 212th day, the moon's 5th; on the Kalends of August, the 213th day, the moon's 7th; on the Nones, the 217th day, the moon's 12th; on the Ides, the 225th day, the moon's 19th. On the day before the Kalends of September, the 243d day, the moon's 7th; on the Kalends of September, the 244th day, the moon's 8th; on the Nones, the 248th day, the moon's 12th; on the Ides, the 256th day, the moon's 20th. On the day before the Kalends of October, the 273d day, the moon's 8th; on the Kalends of October, the 247th day, the moon's 9th; on the Nones, the 280th day, the moon's 15th; on the Ides, the 288th day, the moon's 23d. On the day before the Kalends of November, the 304th day, the moon's 9th; on the Kalends of November, the 305th day, the moon's 10th; on the Nones, the 309th day, the moon's 14th; on the Ides, the

317th day, the moon's 22d. On the day before the Kalends of December, the 334th day, the moon's 10th; on the Kalends of December, the 335th day, the moon's 11th; on the Nones, the 339th day, the moon's 15th; on the Ides, the 347th day, the moon's 23d. On the day before the Kalends of January, the 365th day, the moon's 11th; on the Kalends of January, the 366th day, the moon's 12th.

XIV.
The Paschal or Easter Table of Anatolius.

Now, then, after the reckoning of the days and the exposition of the course of the moon, whereon the whole revolves on to its end, the cycle of the years may be set forth from the commencement. This makes the Passover (Easter season) circulate between the 6th day before the Kalends of April and the 9th before the Kalends of May, according to the following table:

Equinox / Moon / Easter / Moon
1. Sabbath / XXVI. / XVth before the Kalends of May, i.e., 17th April / XVIII.
2. Lord's Day / VII. / Kalends of April, i.e., 1st April / XIV.
3. IId Day (ferial) / XVIII. / XIth before the Kalends of May, i.e., 21st April / XVI.
4. IIId Day / XXIX. / Ides of April, i.e., 13th April / XIX.
5. IVth Day / X. / IVth before the Kalends of April, i.e., 29th March / XIV.
6. Vth Day / XXI. / XIVth before the Kalends of May, i.e., 18th April / XVI.
7. Sabbath / II. / VIth before the Kalends of April, i.e., 27th March / XVII.

8. Lord's Day / XIII. / Kalends of April, i.e., 1st of April / XX.
9. IId Day / XXIV. / XVIIIth before the Kalends of May, i.e., 14th March / XV.
10. IIId Day / V. / VIIIth before the Ides of April, i.e., 6th April / XV.
11. IVth Day / XVI. / IVth before the Kalends of April, i.e., 29th March / XX.
12. Vth Day / XXVII. / IIId before the Ides of April, i.e., 11th April / XV.
13. VIth Day / VIII. / IIId before the Nones of April, i.e., 3rd April / XVII.
14. Sabbath / XX. / IXth before the Kalends of May, i.e., 23rd April / XX.
15. Lord's Day / I. / VIth before the Ides of April, i.e., 8th April / XV.
16. IId Day / XII. / IId before the Kalends of April, i.e., 31st March / XVIII.
17. IVth Day / XXIII. / XIVth before the Kalends of May, i.e., 18th April / XIX.
18. Vth Day / IV. / IId before the Nones of April, i.e., 4th April / XIV.
19. VIth Day / XV. / VIth before the Kalends of April, i.e., 27th March / XVII.

XV.

This cycle of nineteen years is not approved of by certain African investigators who have drawn up larger cycles, because it seems to be somewhat opposed to their surmises and opinions. For these make up the best proved accounts according to their calculation, and determine a certain beginning or certain end for the Easter season, so as that the Paschal festival shall not be celebrated before the eleventh day before the Kalends of April, i.e., 24th March, nor after the moon's twenty-first, and the eleventh day before the Kalends of May, i.e., 21st April. But we hold that these are limits not only not to be followed, but to be detested and overturned. For even in the ancient law it is laid down that this is to be seen to, viz., that the Passover be not celebrated before the transit of the vernal equinox, at which the last of the autumnal *term* is overtaken, on the fourteenth day of the first month, which is one calculated not by the beginnings of the day, but by those of the moon. And as this has been sanctioned by the charge of the Lord, and is in all things accordant with the Catholic faith, it cannot be doubtful to any wise man that to anticipate it must be a thing unlawful and perilous. And, accordingly, this only is it sufficient for all the saints and Catholics to observe, namely, that giving no heed to the diverse opinions of very many, they should keep the solemn festival of the Lord's resurrection within the limits which we have set forth.

XVI.

Furthermore, as to the proposal subjoined to your epistle, that I should attempt to introduce into this little book some notice of the ascent and descent of the sun, which is made out in the distribution of days and nights. The matter proceeds thus: In fifteen days and half an hour, the sun ascending by so many minutes, that is, by four in one day, from the eighth day before the Kalends of January, i.e., 25th December, to the eighth before the Kalends of April, i.e., 25th March, an hour is taken up; at which date there are twelve hours and a twelfth. On this day, towards evening, if it happen also to be the moon's fourteenth, the lamb was sacrificed among the Jews. But if the number went beyond that, so that it was the moon's fifteenth or sixteenth on the evening of the same day, on the fourteenth day of the second moon, in the same month, the Passover was celebrated; and the people ate unleavened bread for seven days, up to the twenty-first day at evening. Hence, if it happens in like manner to us, that the seventh day before the Kalends of April, 26th March, proves to be both the Lord's day and the moon's fourteenth, Easter is to be celebrated on the fourteenth. But if it proves to be the moon's fifteenth or sixteenth, or any day up to the twentieth, then our regard for the Lord's resurrection, which took place on the Lord's day, will lead us to celebrate it on the same principle; yet this should be done so as that the beginning of Easter may not pass beyond the close of their festival, that is to say, the moon's twentieth. And therefore we have said that those parties have committed no trivial offence who have ventured either on anticipating or on going beyond this number, which is given us in the divine Scriptures themselves. And from the eighth day before the Kalends of April, 25th March, to the eighth before the Kalends of July, 24th June, in fifteen days an hour is taken up: the sun ascending every day by two minutes and a half, and the sixth part of a minute. And from the eighth day before the Kalends of July, 24th June, to the eighth before the Kalends of October, 24th September, in like manner, in fifteen days and four hours, an hour is taken up: the sun descending every day by the same number of minutes. And the space remaining on to the eighth day before the Kalends of January, 25th December, is determined in a similar number of hours and minutes. So that thus on the eighth day before the Kalends of January, for the hour there is the hour and half. For up to that day and night are distributed. And the twelve hours which were established at the vernal equinox in the beginning by the Lord's dispensation, being distributed over the night on the eighth before the Kalends of July, the sun ascending through those eighteen several degrees which we have noted, shall be found conjoined with the longer space in the twelfth. And, again, the twelve hours which should be fulfilled at the autumnal equinox in the sun's descent, should be found disjoined on the sixth before the Kalends of January as six hours divided into twelve, the night holding eighteen divided into twelve. And on the eighth before the Kalends of July, in like manner, it held six divided into twelve.

XVII.

Be not ignorant of this, however, that those four determining periods, which we have mentioned, although they are approximated to the Kalends of the following months, yet hold each the middle of a season, viz., of spring and summer, and autumn and winter. And the beginnings of the seasons are not to be fixed at that point at which the Kalends of the month begin. But each season is to be begun in such way that the equinox divides the season of spring from its first day; and the season of summer is divided by the eighth day before the Kalends of July, and that of autumn by the eighth before the Kalends of October, and that of winter by the eighth before the Kalends of January in like manner.

Fragments of the Books on Arithmetic.

What is mathematics?

Aristotle thinks that all philosophy consisted of theory and practice, and divides the practical into ethical and political, and the theoretic again into the theological, the physical, and the mathematical. And thus very clearly and skillfully he shows that mathematics is (a branch of) philosophy.

The Chaldeans were the originators of astronomy, and the Egyptians of geometry and arithmetic....

And whence did mathematics derive its name?

Those of the Peripatetic school affirmed that in rhetoric and poetry, and in the popular music, any one may be an adept though he has gone through no process of study; but that in those pursuits properly called studies, none can have any real knowledge unless he has first become a student of them. Hence they supposed that the theory of these things was called *Mathematics*, from μάθημα, study, science. And the followers of Pythagoras are said to have given this more distinctive name of mathematics to geometry, and arithmetic alone. For of old these had each its own separate name; and they had up till then no name common to both. And he (Archytas) gave them this name, because he found science in them, and that in a manner suitable to man's study. For they (the Pythagoreans) perceived that these studies dealt with things eternal and immutable and perfect, in which things alone they considered that science consisted. But the more recent philosophers have given a more extensive application to this name, so that, in their opinion, the mathematician deals not only with substances incorporeal, and falling simply within the province of the understanding, but also with that which touches upon corporeal and sensible matter. For he ought to be cognizant of the course of the stars, and their velocity, and their magnitudes, and forms, and distances. And, besides, he ought to investigate their dispositions to vision, examining into the causes, why they are not seen as of the same form and of the same size from every distance, retaining, indeed, as we know them to do, their dispositions relative to each other, but producing, at the same time, deceptive appearances, both in respect of order and position. And these are so, either as determined by the state of the heavens and the air, or as seen in reflecting and all polished surfaces and in transparent bodies, and in all similar kinds. In addition to this, they thought that the man ought to be versed in mechanics and geometry and dialectics. And still further, that he should engage himself with the causes of the harmonious combination of sounds, and with the composition of music; which things are bodies, or at least are to be ultimately referred to sensible matter.

What is mathematics?

Mathematics is a theoretic science of things apprehensible by perception and sensation for communication to others. And before this a certain person indulging in a joke, while hitting his mark, said that mathematics is that science to which Homer's description of Discord may be applied.—

"Small at her birth, but rising every hour,
While scarce the skies her horrid (mighty) head can bound, she stalks on earth and shakes the world around."

For it begins with a point and a line, and forthwith it takes heaven itself and all things within its compass.

How many divisions are there of mathematics?

Of the more notable and the earliest mathematics there are two principal divisions, viz., arithmetic and geometry. And of the mathematics which deals with things sensible there are six divisions, viz., computation (practical arithmetic), geodesy, optics, theoretical music, mechanics, and astronomy. But that neither the so-called tactics nor architecture, nor the popular music, nor physics, nor the art which is called equivocally the mechanical, constitutes, as some think, a branch of mathematics, we shall prove, as the discourse proceeds, clearly and systematically.

As to the circle having eight solids and six superficies and four angles...What branches of arithmetic have closest affinity with each other? Computation and theoretical music have a closer affinity than others with arithmetic; for this department, being one also of quantity and ratio, approaches it in number and proportion. Optics and geodesy, again, are more in affinity with geometry. And mechanics and astrology are in general affinity with both.

As to mathematics having its principles in hypothesis and about hypothesis. Now, the term hypothesis is used in three ways, or indeed in many ways. For according to one usage of the term we have the dramatic revolution; and in this sense there are said to be hypotheses in the dramas of Euripides. According to a second meaning, we have the investigation of matters in the special in rhetoric, and in this sense the Sophists say that a hypothesis must be proposed. And, according to a third signification, the beginning of a proof is called a hypothesis, as being the begging of certain matters with a view to the establishment of another in question. Thus it is said that Democritus used a hypothesis, namely, that of atoms and a vacuum; and Asclepiades that of atoms and pores. Now, when applied to mathematics, the term hypothesis is to be taken in the third sense.

That Pythagoras was not the only one who duly honored arithmetic, but that his best known disciples did so too, being wont to say that "all things fit number."

That arithmetic has as its immediate end chiefly the theory of science, than which there is no end either greater or nobler. And its second end is to bring together in one all that is found in determinate substance.

Who among the mathematicians has made any discovery?

Eudemus relates in his *Astrologies* that OEnopides found out the circle of the zodiac and the cycle of the great year. And Thales discovered the eclipse of the sun and its period in the tropics in its constant inequality. And Anaximander discovered that the earth is poised in space, and moves round the axis of the universe. And Anaximenes discovered that the moon has her light from the sun, and found out also the way in which she suffers eclipse. And the rest of the mathematicians have also made additions to these discoveries. We may instance the facts—that the fixed stars move round the axis passing through the poles, while the planets remove from each other round the perpendicular axis of the zodiac; and that the axis of the fixed stars and the planets is the side of a pentedecagon with four-and-twenty parts.

Alexander of Cappadocia.

Translator's Biographical Notice.

[a.d. 170–233–251.] Alexander was at first bishop of a church in Cappadocia, but on his visiting Jerusalem he was appointed to the bishopric of the church there, while the previous bishop Narcissus was alive, in consequence of a vision which was believed to be divine. During the Decian persecution he was thrown into prison at Cæsarea, and died there, a.d. 251. The only writings of his which we know are those from which the extracts are made.

From the Epistles of Alexander.

I. An Epistle to the People of Antioch. Alexander, a servant and prisoner of Jesus Christ, sends greeting in the Lord to the blessed church of Antioch. Easy and light has the Lord made my bonds to me during the time of my imprisonment since I have learned that in the providence of God, Asclepiades—who, in regard to the right faith, is most eminently qualified for the office—has undertaken the episcopate of your holy church of Antioch. And this epistle, my brethren and masters, I have sent by the hand of the blessed presbyter Clement, a man virtuous and well tried, whom ye know already, and will know yet better; who also, coming here by the providence and supervision of the Master, has strengthened and increased the Church of the Lord.

II. From an Epistle to the Antinoites.

Narcissus salutes you, who held the episcopate in this district before me, who is now also my colleague and competitor in prayer for you, and who, having now attained to his hundred and tenth year, unites with me in exhorting you to be of one mind.

III. From an Epistle to Origen.

For this, as thou knows, was the will of God, that the friendship subsisting between us from our forefathers should be maintained unbroken, yea rather, that it should increase in fervency and strength. For we are well acquainted with those blessed fathers who have trodden the course before us, and to whom we too shall soon go: Pantænus, namely, that man verily blessed, my master; and also the holy Clement, who was once my master and my benefactor; and all the rest who may be like them, by whose means also I have come to know thee, my lord and brother, who excels all.

IV. From an Epistle to Demetrius, Bishop of Alexandria.

And he—i.e., *Demetrius*—has added to his letter that this is a matter that was never heard of before, and has never been done now,—namely, that laymen should take part *in public speaking*, when there are bishops present. But in this assertion he has departed evidently far from the truth by some means. For, indeed, wherever there are found persons capable of profiting the brethren, such persons are exhorted by the holy bishops to address the people. Such was the case at Laranda, where Evelpis was thus exhorted by Neon; and at Iconium, Paulinus was thus exhorted by Celsus; and at Synada, Theodorus also by Atticus, our blessed brethren. And it is probable that this is done in other places also, although we know not the fact.

Note by the American Editor.

If Alexander died in the Decian persecution, it is noteworthy how far the sub-apostolic age extended. This contemporary of Cyprian was coadjutor to Narcissus, who may have seen those who knew St. John.

Theognostus of Alexandria.

Translator's Biographical Notice.
[a.d. 260. I can add nothing but conjectures to the following:] Of this Theognostus we have no account by either Eusebius or Jerome. Athanasius, however, mentions him more than once with honor. Thus he speaks of him as ἀνὴρ λόγιος, an *eloquent* or learned man. And again as Θεόγνωστος ὁ θαυμάσιος καὶ σπουδαῖος, the admirable and zealous Theognostus. He seems to have belonged to the Catechetical school of Alexandria, and to have flourished there in the latter half of the third century, probably about a.d. 260. That he was a disciple of Origen, or at least a devoted student of his works, is clear from Photius. He wrote a work in seven books, the title of which is thus given by Photius: *The Outlines of the blessed Theognostus, the exegete of Alexandria.* Dodwell and others are of opinion that by this term *exegete*, is meant the presidency of the Catechetical school and the privilege of public teaching; and that the title, *Outlines*, was taken from Clement, his predecessor in office. According to Photius, the work was on this plan. The first book treated of God the Father, as the maker of the universe; the second, of the necessary existence of the Son; the third, of the Holy Spirit; the fourth, of angels and demons; the fifth and sixth, of the incarnation of God;

while the seventh bore the title, *On God's Creation*. Photius has much to say in condemnation of Thegnostus, who, however, has been vindicated by Bull and Prudentius Maranus. Gregory of Nyssa has also charged him with holding the same error as Eunomius on the subject of the Son's relation to the work of creation. He is adduced, however, by Athanasius as a defender of the Homoüsian doctrine.

From His Seven Books of Hypotyposes or Outlines.

I.

The substance of the Son is not a substance devised extraneously, nor is it one introduced out of nothing; but it was born of the substance of the Father, as the reflection of light or as the steam of water. For the reflection is not the sun itself, and the steam is not the water itself, nor yet again is it anything alien; *neither is He Himself the Father, nor is He alien, but He is* an emanation from the substance of the Father, this substance of the Father suffering the while no partition. For as the sun remains the same and suffers no diminution from the rays that are poured out by it, so neither did the substance of the Father undergo any change in having the Son as an image of itself.

II.

Theognostus, moreover, himself adds words to this effect: He who has offended against the first term and the second, may be judged to deserve smaller punishment; but he who has also despised the third, can no longer find pardon. For by the first term and the second, he says, is meant the teaching concerning the Father and the Son; but by the third is meant the doctrine committed to us with respect to the perfection and the partaking of the Spirit. And with the view of confirming this, he adduces the word spoken by the Savior to the disciples: "I have yet many things to say unto you, but ye cannot bear them now. But when the Holy Spirit is come, He will teach you."

III.

Then he says again: As the Savior converses with those not yet able to receive what is perfect, condescending to their littleness, while the Holy Spirit communes with the perfected, and yet we could never say on that account that the teaching of the Spirit is superior to the teaching of the Son, but only that the Son condescends to the imperfect, while the Spirit is the seal of the perfected; even so it is not on account of the superiority of the Spirit over the Son that the blasphemy against the Spirit is a sin excluding impunity and pardon, but because for the imperfect there is pardon, while for those who have tasted the heavenly gift, and been made perfect, there remains no plea or prayer for pardon.

Pierus of Alexandria.

Translator's Biographical Notice.

[a.d. 275.] Among the very eminent men who flourished near his own time, Eusebius mentions Pierius, a presbyter of Alexandria, and speaks of him as greatly renowned for his voluntary poverty, his philosophical erudition and his skill in the exposition of Scripture and in discoursing to the public assemblies of the Church. He lived in the latter part of the third century, and seems to have been for a considerable period president of the Catechetical school at Alexandria. Jerome says that he was called *Origenes, junior*; and according to Photius, he shared in some of the errors of Origen, on such subjects especially as the doctrine of the Holy Ghost and the pre-existence of souls. In his manner of life he was an ascetic. After the persecution under Galerius or Maximus he lived at Rome. He appears to have devoted himself largely to sacred criticism and the study of the text of Scripture; and among several treatises written by him, and extant in the time of Photius, we find mention made of one on the prophet Hosea. And, in addition to the *Commentary on the First Epistle to the Corinthians*, Photius notices twelve books of his, and praises both their composition and their matter.

I.—A Fragment of a Work of Pierius on the First Epistle of Paul to the Corinthians.

Origen, Dionysius, Pierius, Eusebius of Cæsareia, Didymus, and Apollinaris, have interpreted this epistle most copiously; of whom Pierius, when he was expounding and unfolding the meaning of the apostle, and purposed to explain the words, *For I would that all men were even as I myself*, added this remark: In saying this, Paul, without disguise, preaches celibacy.

II.—A Section on the Writings of Pierius.

Different Discourses of the Presbyter Pierius.

There was read a book by Pierius the presbyter, who, they say, endured the conflict for Christ, along with his brother Isidorus. And he is reputed to have been the teacher of the martyr Pamphilus in ecclesiastical studies, and to have been president of the school at Alexandria. The work contained twelve books. And in style he is perspicuous and clear, with the easy flow, as it were, of a spoken address, displaying no signs of labored art, but bearing us quietly along, smoothly and gently, like off-hand speaking. And in argument he is most fertile, if anyone is so. And he expresses his opinion on many things outside what is now established in the Church, perhaps in an antique manner; but with respect to the Father and the Son, he sets forth his sentiments piously, except that he speaks of two substances and two natures; using, however, the terms substance and nature, as is apparent from what follows, and from what precedes this passage, in the sense of person and not in the sense put on it by the adherents of Arius. With respect to the Spirit, however, he lays down his opinion in a very dangerous and far from pious manner. For he affirms that He is inferior to the Father and the Son in glory. He has a passage also in the book entitled, *On the Gospel according to Luke*, from which it is possible to show that the honor or dishonor of the image is also the honor or dishonor of the original. And, again, he indulges in some obscure speculations, after the manner of the nonsense of Origen, on the subject of the "pre-existence of souls." And also in the book on the Passover (Easter) and on Hosea, he treats both of the cherubim made by Moses, and of the pillar of Jacob, in which passages he admits the actual construction of those things, but propounds the foolish theory that they were given economically, and that they were in no respect like other things which are made;

inasmuch as they bore the likeness of no other form, but had only, as he foolishly says, the appearance of wings.

Theonas of Alexandria.

Translator's Biographical Notice.

[a.d. 300.] Of this Theonas we know extremely little. Eusebius tells us that Maximus, who had held the episcopal office at Alexandria for eighteen years after the death of Dionysius, was succeeded by Theonas. That bishopric, we also learn, he held for nineteen years. His date is fixed as from about 282 to 300 a.d. The only thing of his that has come down to our time is his letter to Lucianus, the chief chamberlain, and a person in high favor with the emperor. This epistle, which is a letter of advice to that individual on the duties of his office, was first published in the *Spicilegium* of Dacherius, and again in Gallandi's *Bibliotheca*. The name of the emperor is not given, neither does the letter itself tell us who the Bishop Theonas was who wrote it. Hence some have, without much reason, supposed another Theonas, bishop of Cyzicus, as the author. And some, such as Cave, have thought the emperor in question was Constantius Chlorus. But the whole circumstances suit Diocletian best. Some infer from the diction of the epistle, as we have it, that it is a translation from a Greek original.

The Epistle of Theonas, Bishop of Alexandria, to Lucianus, the Chief Chamberlain.

Bishop Theonas to Lucianus, the Chief Chamberlain of Our Most Invincible Emperor.

I.

I give thanks to Almighty God and our Lord Jesus Christ, who has not given over the manifesting of His faith throughout the whole world, as the sole specific for our salvation, and the extending of it even in the course of the persecutions of despots. Yea, like gold reduced in the furnace, it has only been made to shine the more under the storms of persecution, and its truth and grandeur have only become always the more and more illustrious, so that now, peace being granted to the churches by our gracious prince, the works of Christians are shining even in sight of the unbelieving, and God your Father, who is in heaven, is glorified thereby; a thing which, if we desire to be Christians in deed rather than in word, we ought to seek and aspire after as our first object on account of our salvation. For if we seek our own glory, we set our desire upon a vain and perishing object, and one which leads ourselves on to death. But the glory of the Father and of the Son, who for our salvation was nailed to the cross, makes us safe for the everlasting redemption; and that is the greatest hope of Christians. Wherefore, my Lucianus, I neither suppose nor desire that you should make it a matter of boasting, that by your means many persons belonging to the palace of the emperor have been brought to the knowledge of the truth; but rather does it become us to give the thanks to our God who has made thee a good instrument for a good work, and has raised thee to great honor with the emperor, that you might diffuse the sweet savor of the Christian name to His own glory and to the salvation of many. For just the more completely that the emperor himself, though not yet attached to the Christian religion, has entrusted the care of his life and person to these same Christians as his more faithful servants, so much the more careful ought ye to be, and the more diligent and watchful in seeing to his safety and in attending upon him, so that the name of Christ may be greatly glorified thereby, and His faith extended daily through you who wait upon the emperor. For in old times some former princes thought us malevolent and filled with all manner of crime; but now, seeing your good works, they should not be able to avoid glorifying Christ Himself.

II.

Therefore you ought to strive to the utmost of your power not to fall into a base or dishonorable, not to say an absolutely flagitious way of thinking, lest the name of Christ be thus blasphemed even by you. Be it far from you that you should sell the privilege of access to the emperor to any one for money, or that you should by any means place a dishonest account of any affair before your prince, won over either by prayers or by bribes. Let all the lust of avarice be put from you, which serves the cause of idolatry rather than the religion of Christ. No filthy lucre, no duplicity, can befit the Christian who embraces the simple and unadorned Christ. Let no scurrilous or base talk have place among you. Let all things be done with modesty, courteousness, affability, and uprightness, so that the name of our God and Lord Jesus Christ may be glorified in all.

Discharge the official duties to which you are severally appointed with the utmost fear of God and affection to your prince, and perfect carefulness. Consider that every command of the emperor which does not offend God has proceeded from God Himself; and execute it in love as well as in fear, and with all cheerfulness. For there is nothing which so well refreshes a man who is wearied out with weighty cares as the seasonable cheerfulness and benign patience of an intimate servant; nor, again, on the other hand, does anything so much annoy and vex him as the moroseness and impatience and grumbling of his servant. Be such things far from you Christians, whose walk is in zeal for the faith. But in order that God may be honored in yourselves, suppress you and tread down all your vices of mind and body. Be clothed with patience and courtesy; be replenished with the virtues and the hope of Christ. Bear all things for the sake of your Creator Himself; endure all things; overcome and get above all things, that ye may win Christ the Lord. Great are these duties, and full of painstaking. But he that strives for the mastery is temperate in all things; and they do it to obtain a corruptible crown, but we an incorruptible.

III.

But because, as I apprehend it, ye are assigned to different offices, and you, Lucianus, are styled the head of them all, whom, also, by the grace of Christ given you, you are able to direct and dispose in their different spheres, I am certain that it will not displease you if I also bring before your notice, in a particular and summary manner, some of my sentiments on the subject of these offices. For I hear that one of you keeps the private moneys of the emperor; another the imperial robes and ornaments; another the precious vessels; another the books, who, I understand, does not as yet belong to the believers; and others the different parts of the household goods. And in what manner, therefore, these charges ought, in my judgment, to be executed, I shall indicate in a few words.

IV.

He who has charge of the private moneys of the emperor ought to keep everything in an exact reckoning. He should be ready at any time to give an accurate account of all things. He should note down everything in writing, if it is at all possible, before giving money to another. He should never trust such things to his memory, which, being drawn off day by day to other matters, readily fails us, so that, without writing, we sometimes honestly certify things which have never existed; neither should this kind of writing be of a commonplace order, but such as easily and clearly unfolds all things, and leaves the mind of the inquirer without any scruple or doubt on the subject; a thing which will easily be effected if a distinct and separate account is kept in writing of all receipts, and of the time when, and the person by whom, and the place at which they were made. And, in like manner, all that is paid out to others, or expended by order of the emperor, should be entered in its own place by itself in the reckoning; and that servant should be faithful and prudent, so that his lord may rejoice that he has set him over his goods, and may glorify Christ in him.

V.

Nor will the diligence and care of that servant be less who has the custody of the robes and imperial ornaments. All these he should enter in a most exact catalogue, and he should keep a note of what they are and of what sort, and in what places stored, and when he received them, and from whom, and whether they are soiled or unsoiled. All these things he should keep in his diligence; he should often review again, and he should often go over them that they may be the more readily known again. All these he should have at hand, and all in readiness; and he should always give the clearest information on every matter on which it is sought, to his prince or his superior, whenever they ask about anything; and all this at the same time in such wise that everything may be done in humility and cheerful patience, and that the name of Christ may be praised even in a small matter.

VI.

In a similar manner should he conduct himself to whose fidelity are entrusted the vessel of silver and gold, and crystal or murrha, for eating or for drinking? All these he should arrange suitably, of them all he should keep an account, and with all diligence he should make an inventory of how many and which sort of precious stones are in them. He should examine them all with great prudence; he should produce them in their proper places and on their proper occasions. And he should observe most carefully to whom he gives them, and at what time, and from whom he receives them again, lest there should occur any mistake or injurious suspicion, or perhaps some considerable loss in things of value.

VII.

The most responsible person, however, among you, and also the most careful, will be he who may be entrusted by the emperor with the custody of his library. He will himself select for this office a person of proved knowledge, a man grave and adapted to great affairs, and ready to reply to all applications for information, such a one as Philadelphus chose for this charge, and appointed to the superintendence of his most noble library—I mean

Aristeus, his confidential chamberlain, whom he sent also as his legate to Eleazar, with most magnificent gifts, in recognition of the translation of the Sacred Scriptures; and this person also wrote the full history of the Seventy Interpreters. If, therefore, it should happen that a believer in Christ is called to this same office, he should not despise that secular literature and those Gentile intellects which please the emperor. To be praised are the poets for the greatness of their genius, the acuteness of their inventions, the aptness and lofty eloquence of their style. To be praised are the orators; to be praised also are the philosophers in their own class. To be praised, too, are the historians, who unfold to us the order of exploits, and the manners and institutions of our ancestors, and show us the rule of life from the proceedings of the ancients. On occasion also he will endeavor to laud the divine Scriptures, which, with marvelous care and most liberal expenditure, Ptolemy Philadelphus caused to be translated into our language; and sometimes, too, the Gospel and the Apostle will be lauded for their divine oracles; and there will be an opportunity for introducing the mention of Christ; and, little by little, His exclusive divinity will be explained; and all these things may happily come to pass by the help of Christ.

    He ought, therefore, to know all the books which the emperor possesses; he should often turn them over, and arrange them neatly in their proper order by catalogue; if, however, he shall have to get new books, or old ones transcribed, he should be careful to obtain the most accurate copyists; and if that cannot be done, he should appoint learned men to the work of correction, and recompense them justly for their labors. He should also cause all manuscripts to be restored according to their need, and should embellish them, not so much with mere superstitious extravagance, as with useful adornment; and therefore he should not aim at having the whole manuscripts written on purple skins and in letters of gold, unless the emperor has specially required that. With the utmost submission, however, he should do everything that is agreeable to Cæsar. As he is able, he should, with all modesty, suggest to the emperor that he should read, or hear read, those books which suit his rank and honor, and minister to good use rather than to mere pleasure. He should himself first be thoroughly familiar with those books, and he should often commend them in presence of the emperor, and set forth, in an appropriate fashion, the testimony and the weight of those who approve them, that he may not seem to lean to his own understanding only.

VIII.

Those, moreover, who have the care of the emperor's person should be in all things as prompt as possible; always, as we have said, cheerful in countenance, sometimes merry, but ever with such perfect modesty as that he may commend it above all else in you all, and perceive that it is the true product of the religion of Christ. You should also all be elegant and tidy in person and attire, yet, at the same time, not in such wise as to attract notice by extravagance or affectation, lest Christian modesty be scandalized. Let everything be ready at its proper time, and disposed as well as possible in its own order. There should also be due arrangement among you, and carefulness that no confusion appear in your work, nor any loss of property in any way; and appropriate places should be settled and suitably prepared, in accordance with the capacity (*captu*) and importance of the places.

Besides this, your servants should be the most thoroughly honest, and circumspect, and modest, and as serviceable to you as possible. And see that you instruct and teach them in true doctrine with all the patience and charity of Christ; but if they despise and lightly esteem your instructions, then dismiss them, lest their wickedness by any hap recoil upon yourselves. For sometimes we have seen, and often we have heard, how masters have been held in ill repute in consequence of the wickedness of their servants.

If the emperor visits her imperial majesty, or she him, then should ye also be most circumspect in eye and demeanor, and in all your words. Let her mark your mastery of yourselves and your modesty; and let her followers and attendants mark *your demeanor*; let them mark it and admire it, and by reason thereof praise Jesus Christ our Lord in you. Let your conversation always be temperate and modest, and seasoned with religion as with salt. And, further, let there be no jealousy among you or contentiousness, which might bring you into all manner of confusion and division, and thus also make you objects of aversion to Christ and to the emperor, and lead you into the deepest abomination, so that not one stone of your building could stand upon another.

IX.

And do thou, my dearest Lucianus, since thou art wise, bear with good-will the unwise; and they too may perchance become wise. Do no one an injury at any time, and provoke no one to anger. If an injury is done to you, look to Jesus Christ; and even as ye desire that He may remit your transgressions, do ye also forgive them theirs; and then also shall ye do away with all ill-will, and bruise the head of that ancient serpent, who is ever on the watch with all subtlety to undo your good works and your prosperous attainments. Let no day pass by without reading some portion of the Sacred Scriptures, at such convenient hour as offers, and giving some space to meditation. And never cast off the habit of reading in the Holy Scriptures; for nothing feeds the soul and enriches the mind so well as those sacred studies do. But look to this as the chief gain you are to make by them, that, in all due patience, ye may discharge the duties of your office religiously and piously— that is, in the love of Christ— and despise all transitory objects for the sake of His eternal promises, which in truth surpass all human comprehension and understanding, and shall conduct you into everlasting felicity.

A happy adieu to you in Christ, my Lord Lucianus.

Phileas.

Translator's Biographical Notice.

[a.d. 307.] From Jerome we learn that this Phileas belonged to Thmuis, a town of Lower Egypt, the modern *Tmai*, which was situated between the Tanite and Mendesian branches of the Nile, an episcopal seat, and in the time of Valentinian and Theodosius the Great a place of considerable consequence, enjoying a separate government of its own. Eusebius speaks of him as a man not less distinguished for his services to his country than for his eminence in philosophical studies and his proficiency in foreign literature and science. He tells us further, that, along with another person of considerable importance, by name Philoromus, being brought to trial for his faith, he withstood the threats and insults of the judge, and all the entreaties of relatives and friends, to compromise his Christian belief, and was condemned to lose his head. Jerome also, in the passage already referred to, names him a *true philosopher, and, at the same time, a godly martyr;* and states, that *on assuming the bishopric of his native district, he wrote a very, elegant book in praise of the martyrs.* Of this book certain fragments are preserved for us in Eusebius. In addition to these we have also an epistle which the same Phileas seems to have written in the name of three other bishops, as well as himself, to Meletius, the bishop of Lycopolis, and founder of the Meletian schism. This epistle appears to have been written in Greek; but we possess only a Latin version, which, however, from its abrupt style, is believed to be very ancient. The four bishops whose names stand at the head of the Epistle—viz., Hesychius, Pachomius, Theodorus, and Phileas, are also mentioned by Eusebius (*Hist. Eccl.*, viii. 13) as distinguished martyrs. This epistle was written evidently when those bishops were in prison, and its date is determined by the mention of Peter as the then bishop of Alexandria. The martyrdom of Phileas is fixed with much probability as happening at Alexandria, under Maximus, about the year 307 a.d.

Fragments of the Epistle of Phileas to the People of Thmuis.

I.

Having before them all these examples and signs and illustrious tokens which are given us in the divine and holy Scriptures, the blessed martyrs who lived with us did not hesitate, but, directing the eye of their soul in sincerity to that God who is over all, and embracing with willing mind the death which their piety cost them, they adhered steadfastly to their vocation. For they learned that our Lord Jesus Christ endured man's estate on our behalf, that He might destroy all sin, and furnish us with the provision needful for our entrance into eternal life. "For He thought it not robbery to be equal with God: but made Himself of no reputation, taking upon Him the form of a servant: and being found in fashion as a man, He humbled Himself unto death, even the death of the cross." For which reason also these Christ-bearing martyrs sought zealously the greater gifts, and endured, some of them, every kind of pain and all the varied contrivances of torture not merely once, but once and again; and though the guards showed their fury against them not only by threatening in word, but also by deeds of violence, they did not swerve from their resolution, because *perfect love casted out fear.*

II.
And to narrate their virtue and their manly endurance under every torment, what language would suffice? For as everyone who chose was at liberty to abuse them, some beat them with wooden clubs, and others with rods, and others with scourges, and others again with thongs, and others with ropes. And the spectacle of these modes of torture had great variety in it, and exhibited vast malignity. For some had their hands bound behind them, and were suspended on the rack and had every limb in their body stretched with a certain kind of pulleys. Then after all this the torturers, according to their orders, lacerated with the sharp iron claws the whole

body, not merely, as in the case of murderers, the sides only, but also the stomach and the knees and the cheeks. And others were hung up in mid-air, suspended by one hand from the portico, and their sufferings were fiercer than any other kind of agony by reason of the distention of their joints and limbs. And others were bound to pillars, face to face, not touching the ground with their feet, but hanging with all the weight of the body, so that their chains were drawn all the more tightly by reason of the tension. And this they endured not simply as long as the governor spoke with them, or had leisure to hear them, but well-nigh through the whole day. For when he passed on to others he left some of those under his authority to keep watch over these former, and to observe whether any of them, being overcome by the torture, seemed likely to yield. But he gave them orders at the same time to cast them into chains without sparing, and thereafter, when they were expiring, to throw them on the ground and drag them along. For they said that they would not give themselves the slightest concern about us, but would look upon us and deal with us as if we were nothing at all. This second mode of torture our enemies devised then over and above the scourging.

III.

And there were also some who, after the tortures, were placed upon the stocks and had both their feet stretched through all the four holes, so that they were compelled to lie on their back on the stocks, as they were unable (to stand) in consequence of the fresh wounds they had over the whole body from the scourging. And others being thrown upon the ground lay prostrated there by the excessively frequent application of the tortures; in which condition they exhibited to the onlookers a still more dreadful spectacle than they did when actually undergoing their torments, bearing, as they did, on their bodies the varied and manifold tokens of the cruel ingenuity of their tortures. While this state of matters went on, some died under their tortures, putting the adversary to shame by their constancy. And others were thrust half-dead into the prison, where in a few days, worn out with their agonies, they met their end. But the rest, getting sure recovery under the application of remedies, through time and their lengthened detention in prison, became more confident. And thus then, when they were commanded to make their choice between these alternatives, namely, either to put their hand to the unholy sacrifice and thus secure exemption from further trouble, and obtain from them their abominable sentence of absolution and liberation, or else to refuse to sacrifice, and thus expect the judgment of death to be executed on them, they never hesitated, but went cheerfully to death. For they knew the sentence declared for us of old by the Holy Scriptures: "He that sacrifices to other gods," it is said, "shall be utterly destroyed." And again "Thou shalt have no other gods before Me."

The Epistle of the Same Phileas of Thmuis to Meletius, Bishop of Lycopolis.

The Beginning of the Epistle of the Bishops.

Hesychius, Pachomius, Theodorus, and Phileas, to Meletius, our friend and fellow minister in the Lord, greeting. Some reports having reached us concerning thee, which, on the testimony of certain individuals who came to us, spoke of certain things foreign to divine order and ecclesiastical rule which are being attempted, yea, rather which are being done by thee, we, in an ingenuous manner held them to be untrustworthy, regarding them to be such as we would not willingly credit, when we thought of the audacity implied in their magnitude and their uncertain attempts. But since many who are visiting us at the present time have lent some credibility to these reports, and have not hesitated to attest them as facts, we, to our exceeding surprise, have been compelled to indite this letter to thee. And what agitation and sadness have been caused to us all in common and to each of us individually by (the report of) the ordination carried through by thee in parishes having no manner of connection with thee, we are unable sufficiently to express. We have not delayed, however, by a short statement to prove your practice wrong. There is the law of our fathers and forefathers, of which neither art thou thyself ignorant, established according to divine and ecclesiastical order; for it is all for the good pleasure of God and the zealous regard of better things. By them it has been established and settled that it is not lawful for any bishop to celebrate ordinations in other parishes than his own; a law which is exceedingly important and wisely devised. For, in the first place, it is but right that the conversation and life of those who are ordained should be examined with great care; and in the second place, that all confusion and turbulence should be done away with. For every one shall have enough to do in managing his own parish, and in finding with great care and many anxieties suitable subordinates *among these* with whom he has passed his whole life, and who have been trained under his hands. But thou, neither making any account of these things, nor regarding the future, nor considering the law of our sainted fathers and those who have been taken to Christ time after time, nor the honor of our great bishop and father, Peter, on whom we all depend in the hope which we have in the Lord Jesus Christ, nor softened by our imprisonments and trials, and daily and multiplied reproach, hast ventured on subverting all things at once. And what means will be left thee for justifying thyself with respect to these things? But perhaps thou wilt say: I did this to prevent many being drawn away with the unbelief of many, because the flocks were in need and forsaken, there being no pastor with them. Well, but it is most certain that they are not in such destitution: in the first place, because there are many going about them and in a position to act as visitors; and in the second place, even if there was some measure of neglect on their side, then the proper way would have been for the representation to be made promptly by the people, and for us to take account of them according to their desert. But they knew that they were in no want of ministers, and therefore they did not come to seek them. They knew that we were wont to discharge them with an admonition from such inquisition for matter of complaint, or that everything was done with all carefulness which seemed to be for their profit; for all was done under correction, and all was considered with well-approved honesty. Thou, however, giving such strenuous attention to the deceits of certain parties and their vain words, hast made a stealthy leap to the celebrating of ordinations. For if, indeed, those with thee were constraining thee to this, and in their ignorance were doing violence to ecclesiastical order, thou ought to have followed the common rule and have informed us by letter; and in that way what seemed expedient would have been done. And if perchance some persuaded you to credit their story that it was all over with us,—a thing of which thou could not have been ignorant, because there were many passing and repassing by us who might visit you,—even although, I say, this had been the case, yet thou ought to have waited for the judgment of the superior father and for his allowance of this practice. But without giving any heed to these matters, but indulging a different expectation, yea rather, indeed, denying all respect to us, thou hast provided certain rulers for the people. For now we have learned, too, that there were also divisions, because thy unwarrantable exercise of the right of ordination displeased many. And thou wert not persuaded to delay such procedure or restrain thy purpose readily even by the word of the Apostle Paul, the most blessed seer, and the man who put on Christ, who is the Christ of all of us no less; for he, in writing to his dearly-beloved son Timothy, says: "Lay hands suddenly on no man, neither be partaker of other men's sins." And thus he at once shows his own anxious consideration for him, and gives him his example and exhibits the law according to which, with all carefulness and caution, parties are to be chosen for the honor of ordination. We make this declaration to thee that in future thou may study to keep within the safe and salutary limits of the law.

The Conclusion of the Epistle of the Bishops.

After receiving and perusing this epistle, he neither wrote any reply nor repaired to them in the prison, nor went to the blessed Peter. But when all these bishops and presbyters and deacons had suffered martyrdom in the prison at Alexandria, he at once entered Alexandria. Now in that city there was a certain person, by name Isidorus, turbulent in character, and possessed with the ambition of being a teacher. And there was also a certain Arius, who wore the habit of piety, and was in like manner possessed with the ambition to be a teacher. And when they discovered the object of Meletius's passion and what it was that he sought, hastening to him, and looking with an evil eye on the episcopal authority of the blessed Peter, that the aim and desire of Meletius might be made patent, they discovered to Meletius certain presbyters, then in hiding, to whom the blessed Peter had given power to act as parish-visitors. And Meletius recommending them to improve the opportunity given them for rectifying their error, suspended them for the time, and by his own authority ordained two persons in their place, namely, one in prison and another in the mines. On learning these things the blessed Peter, with much endurance, wrote to the people of Alexandria an epistle in the following terms.

Pamphilus.
_____

Translator's Biographical Notice.

[a.d. 309.] According to the common account Pamphilus was a native of Berytus, the modern Beirût, and a member of a distinguished Phoenician family. Leaving Berytus, however, at an early period, he repaired to Alexandria and studied under Pierius, the well-known head of the Catechetical school there. At a subsequent period he went to the Palestinian Cæsareia, and was made a presbyter of the Church there under Bishop Agapius. In course of the persecutions of Diocletian he was thrown into prison by Urbanus, the governor of Palestine. This took place towards the end of the year 307 a.d., and his confinement lasted till the beginning of the year 309, when he suffered martyrdom by order of Firmilianus, who had succeeded Urbanus in the governorship of the country. During his imprisonment he enjoyed the affectionate attendance of Eusebius, the Church historian, and the tender friendship which subsisted long between the two is well known. It was as a memorial of that intimacy that Eusebius took the surname of Pamphili. Pamphilus appears to have given himself up with great enthusiasm to the promotion of Biblical studies, and is spoken of as the founder of a theological school in which special importance was attached to exposition. He busied himself also with the transcription and dissemination of the Scriptures and other writings, such as those of Origen, of whom he was a devoted follower. At Cæsareia he established a great public library, consisting mainly of ecclesiastical writers; and among the treasures of that library are mentioned the *Tetrapla* and *Hexapla* of Origen, from which, with the help of Eusebius, he produced a new and revised edition of the Septuagint. There is a statement in Jerome to the effect that, though he was so great a student of the writings of others, Pamphilus, through an excess of modesty, wrote no work of his own, with exception of some letters to his friends. But there is a work bearing the title of *An Exposition of the Chapters of the Acts of the Apostles*, which is attributed by many to him, although others ascribe it to Euthalius, bishop of Sulce. And besides this there is also the *Apology for Origen*, of which, according to the statement of Photius, the first five books were compiled by Pamphilus, in conjunction with Eusebius, during the period of his imprisonment, the sixth book being added by Eusebius after his friend's martyrdom. Of this *Apology* we possess now only the first book, and that, too, only in the faulty Latin version of Rufinus. There are repeated und warmly eulogistic references to Pamphilus in the *Ecclesiastical History* of Eusebius. Thus he speaks of him as *that holy martyr of our day*; and as *that most eloquent man, and that philosopher truly such in his life*; and again, as *that most admirable man of our times, that glory of the church of Cæsareia.* He devotes the eleventh chapter of the eighth book also to a notice of Pamphilus and other martyrs. And besides all this he wrote a separate life of his friend, in three books, of which, however, all has perished, with exception of a few disputed fragments.

An Exposition of the Chapters of the Acts of the Apostles.

Having had ourselves the advantage of the method and model received from our fathers and teachers, we attempt, in a modest way, to give these in this exposition of the chapters, entreating your forgiveness for the rashness of such an endeavor in us who are young in point both of years and of study, and looking to have the indulgence of everyone who reads this writing in prayer on our behalf. We make this exposition, therefore, after the history of Luke, the evangelist and historian. And, accordingly, we have indicated whole chapters by the letters of the alphabet, and their subdivisions into parts we have noted by means of the asterisk.

A. Of Christ's teaching after His resurrection, and of His appearing to the disciples, and of the promise of the gift of the Holy Ghost, and of the spectacle and manner of Christ's assumption.

B. Peter's discourse to those who were made disciples, on the subject of the death and reprobation of Judas; in this chapter we have also the section on the substitution of Matthias, who was elected by lot through the grace of God with prayer.

C. Of the divine descent of the Holy Ghost on the day of Pentecost which lighted on them who believed. In this we have also the instruction delivered by Peter, and passages from the prophets on the subject, and on the passion and resurrection and assumption of Christ, and the gift of the Holy Ghost; also of the faith of those present, and their salvation by baptism; and, further, of the unity of spirit pervading the believers and promoting the common good, and of the addition made to their number.

D. Of the healing in (the name of) Christ of the man lame from his birth; and of the discourse of Peter, in which he reasons and sympathizes and counsels with respect to his salvation. And here we have the interposition of the chief priests through jealousy of what had taken place, and their judgment on the miracle, and Peter's confession of the power and grace of Christ. Also the section on the unbelieving chief priests, commanding that they should not speak boldly in the name of Christ, and of the dismissal of the apostles. Then * the thanksgivings offered up by the Church for the faithful constancy of the apostles.

E. Of the harmonious and universal fellowship of the believers; and also of Ananias and Sapphira and their miserable end.

F. Of the apostles being cast into prison, and led out of it by night by the angel of the Lord, who enjoined them to preach Jesus without restraint; and of the fact that, on the following day, the chief priests apprehended them again, and, after scourging them, sent them away with the charge not to teach any longer. Then the trusty opinion of Gamaliel touching the apostles, together with certain examples and proofs.

G. Of the election of the seven deacons.

H. The rising and slanderous information of the Jews against Stephen, and his address concerning the covenant of God with Abraham, and concerning the twelve patriarchs. Also the account of the famine and the buying of corn, and the mutual recognition of the sons of Jacob, and of the birth of Moses and the appearance of God to Moses, which took place at Mount Sinai. Also of the exodus and calf-making of Israel (and other matters), up to the times of Solomon and the building of the temple. Then the acknowledgment of the super celestial glory of Jesus Christ which was revealed to Stephen himself, on account of which Stephen was himself stoned, and fell asleep piously.

I. Of the persecution of the Church and the burial of Stephen; also of the healing of many in Samaria by Philip the apostle.

J. Of Simon Magus, who believed and was baptized with many others; also of the sending of Peter and John to them, and their praying for the descent of the Holy Ghost upon the baptized.

K. That the participation of the Holy Ghost was not given for money, nor to hypocrites, but to saints by faith; also of the hypocrisy and the reproof of Simon.

L. That the Lord helps the good and the believing on the way to salvation, as is shown from the instance of the eunuch.

M. Of the divine call that came from heaven for Paul to the apostleship of Christ; also of the healing and the baptism of Paul by the hand of Ananias, in accordance with the revelation from God, and of his boldness of speech and his association with the apostles by the instrumentality of Barnabas.

N. Of the paralytic Æneas who was cured by Peter at Lydda. Also the account of Tabitha, the friend of widows, whom Peter raised from the dead by means of prayer in Joppa.

O. Of Cornelius, and what the angel said to him. Also what was spoken to Peter from heaven with respect to the calling of the Gentiles. Then that Peter, on being summoned, came to Cornelius. The repetition by Cornelius of the things which the angel said to Cornelius himself. Peter's instruction of them in Christ, and the gift of τ'ε Holy Ghost upon those who heard him, and how those who believed from among the Gentiles were baptized there.

P. That Peter recounts to the apostles who contended with him all the things that had happened in order and separately. Then the sending of Barnabas to the brethren in Antioch.

Q. The prophecy of Agabus respecting the famine in the world, and the liberal relief sent to the brethren in Jerusalem.

R. The slaying of the Apostle James. Also the apprehension of Peter by Herod, and the account of the manner in which the angel by divine command delivered him from his bonds, and how Peter, after showing himself to the disciples by night, quietly withdrew. Also of the punishment of the keepers, and then of the miserable and fatal overthrow of the impious Herod.

S. The sending of Barnabas and Paul by the Holy Ghost to Cyprus. The things which he did there in the name of Christ on Elymas the sorcerer.

T. Paul's admirable exposition of the truth concerning Christ, both from the law and from the prophets in their order, both historical and evangelical; his use both of the confuting and the argumentative mode of discourse on the subject of the transference of the word of preaching to the Gentiles, and of their persecution and their arrival at Iconium.

U. How, when they had preached Christ in Iconium, and many had believed, the apostles were persecuted.

V. Of the man lame from his birth in Lystra who was healed by the apostles; on account of which they were taken by the people of the place for gods who had appeared on earth. After that, however, Paul is stoned there by the neighboring people.

W. That according to the decree and judgment of the apostles, the Gentiles who believe ought not to be circumcised. Here, also, is the epistle of the apostles themselves to those from among the Gentiles, on the subject of the things from which they should keep themselves. The dissension of Paul with Barnabas on account of Mark.

X. Of the teaching of Timothy, and of the coming of Paul into Macedonia according to revelation. Of the faith and salvation of a certain woman Lydia, and of the cure of the damsel having a spirit of divination, on account of which the masters of the damsel cast Paul into prison; and of the earthquake and miracle which happened there; and how the jailer believed and was baptized forthwith that same night with all his house. That the apostles on being besought went out from the prison.

Y. Of the tumult that arose in Thessalonica on account of their preaching, and of the flight of Paul to Berea, and thence to Athens.

Z. Of the inscription on the altar at Athens, and of the philosophic preaching and piety of Paul.

AA. Of Aquila and Priscilla, and the unbelief of the Corinthians, and of the good-will of God towards them according to fore-knowledge revealed to Paul. Also of Priscus, the chief ruler of the synagogue, who believed with certain others and was baptized. And that a tumult being stirred up in Corinth, Paul departed; and coming to Ephesus, and having discoursed there, he left it. And concerning Apollos, an eloquent man and a believer.

BB. Of baptism and the gift of the Holy Ghost conferred by means of the prayer of Paul on those who believed in Ephesus, and of the healing of the people. Of the sons of Sceva, and as to its not being meet to approach those who have become unbelieving and unworthy of the faith; and of the confession of those who believed; and of the tumult that was stirred up in Ephesus by Demetrius, the silversmith, against the apostles.

CC. Of the circuit of Paul, in which also we have the account of the death of Eutychus and his restoration by prayer in Troas; also Paul's own pastoral exhortations to the presbyters at Ephesus; also Paul's voyage from Ephesus to Cæsareia in Palestine.

DD. The prophecy of Agabus as to what should befall Paul in Jerusalem.

EE. The address of James to Paul touching the matter that he should not offer to keep the Hebrews back from the practice of circumcision.

FF. Of the tumult that was excited against Paul in Jerusalem, and how the chief-captain rescues him from the mob. Also Paul's speech concerning himself and his vocation to be an apostle; and of what Ananias said to Paul in Damascus, and of the vision and the voice of God that befell him once in the temple. And that when Paul was about to be beaten for these words, on declaring that he was a Roman, he was let go.

GG. What Paul endured, and what he said, and what he did exactly when he came down into the council.

HH. Of the ambush planned by the Jews against Paul, and its discovery to Lysias; and that Paul was sent to Cæsareia to the governor with soldiers and with a letter.

II. Of the accusation laid by Tertullus in Paul's case, and of his defense of himself before the governor.

JJ. Of the removal of Felix and the arrival of Festus as his successor, and of Paul's pleading before them, and his dismissal.

KK. The coming of Agrippa and Bernice, and their inquiry into the case of Paul. Paul's defense of himself before Agrippa and Bernice, respecting his nurture in the law, and his vocation to the Gospel. That Paul does no wrong to the Jews, Agrippa said to Festus.

LL. Paul's voyage to Rome, abounding in very many and very great perils. Paul's exhortation to those with him as to his hope of deliverance. The shipwreck of Paul, and how they effected their safety on the island of Melita, and what marvelous things he did on it.

MM. How Paul reached Rome from Melita.

NN. Of Paul's discourse with the Jews in Rome.

There are in all forty chapters; and the sections following these, and marked with the asterisk, are forty-eight.

Malchion.
_____

Translator's Biographical Notice.

[a.d. 270.] Eusebius speaks of Malchion as a man accomplished in other branches of learning and well-versed in Greek letters in particular, and as holding the presidency of the Sophists' school at Antioch. Jerome1390 says that he taught rhetoric most successfully in the same city. Nor was it only that he excelled in secular erudition; but for the earnest sincerity of his Christian faith he obtained the dignity of presbyter in the church of that place, as Eusebius also tells us. He took part in the Synod of Antioch, which Eusebius calls the final council, and which Gallandi and others call the *second*, in opposition to Pearson, who holds that there was but one council at Antioch. This synod met apparently about a.d. 269, and dealt with Paul of Samosata, who had introduced the heresy of Artemon into the church of Antioch; and Eusebius says that Malchion was the only one who, in the discussion which took place there with the arch-heretic, and which was taken down by stenographers who were present, was able to detect the subtle and crafty sentiments of the man. Paul's real opinions being thus unveiled, after he had baffled the acuteness of his ecclesiastical judges for some time, he was at length convicted; and the discussion was published, and a synodical epistle was sent on the subject to Dionysius, bishop of Rome, and to Maximus of Alexandria, and to all the provinces, which, according to Jerome (*De vir. illustr.*, ch. 71), was written by Malchion, and of which we have extracts in Eusebius.

Anatolius and Minor Writers

I.—The Epistle Written by Malchion, In Name of the Synod of Antioch, Against Paul of Samosata.

To Dionysius and Maximus, and to all our fellows in the ministry throughout the world, both bishops and presbyters and deacons, and to the whole Catholic Church under heaven, Helenus and Hymenæus and Theophilus and Theotecnus and Maximus, Proclus, Nicomas, and Ælianus, and Paul and Bolanus and Protogenes and Hierax and Eutychius and Theodorus and Malchion and Lucius, and all the others who are with us, dwelling in the neighboring cities and nations, both bishops and presbyters and deacons, together with the churches of God, send greeting to our brethren beloved in the Lord.

1. After some few introductory words, they proceed thus:—We wrote to many of the bishops, even those who live at a distance, and exhorted them to give their help in relieving us from this deadly doctrine; among these, we addressed, for instance, Dionysius, the bishop of Alexandria, and Firmilian of Cappadocia, those men of blessed name. Of these, the one wrote to Antioch without even deigning to honor the leader in this error by addressing him; nor did he write to him in his own name, but to the whole district, of which letter we have also subjoined a copy. And Firmilian, who came twice in person, condemned the innovations in doctrine, as we who were present know and bear witness, and as many others know as well as we. But when he (Paul) promised to give up these opinions, he believed him; and hoping that, without any reproach to the Word, the matter would be rightly settled, he postponed his decision; in which action, however, he was deceived by that denier of his

God and Lord, and betrayer of the faith which he formerly held. And now Firmilian was minded to cross to Antioch; and he came as far as Tarsus, as having already made trial of the man's infidel iniquity. But when we had just assembled, and were calling for him and waiting for his arrival, his end came upon him.

2. After other matters again, they tell us in the following terms of what manner of life he was:—But there is no need of judging his actions when he was outside (the Church), when he revolted from the faith and turned aside to spurious and illegitimate doctrines.

Nor need we say anything of such matters as this, that, whereas he was formerly poor and beggarly, having neither inherited a single possession from his fathers, nor acquired any property by art or by any trade, he has now come to have excessive wealth by his deeds of iniquity and sacrilege, and by those means by which he despoils and concusses the brethren, casting the injured unfairly in their suit, and promising to help them for a price, yet deceiving them all the while and to their loss, taking advantage of the readiness of those in difficulties to give in order to get deliverance from what troubled them, and thus supposing that gain is godliness. Neither need I say anything about his pride and the haughtiness with which he assumed worldly dignities, and his wishing to be styled procurator rather than bishop, and his strutting through the market-places, and reading letters and reciting them as he walked in public, and his being escorted by multitudes of people going before him and following him; so that he brought ill-will and hatred on the faith by his haughty demeanor and by the arrogance of his heart. Nor shall I say anything of the quackery which he practices in the ecclesiastical assemblies, in the way of courting popularity and making a great parade, and astounding by such arts the minds of the less sophisticated; nor of his setting up for himself a lofty tribunal and throne, so unlike a disciple of Christ; nor of his having a secretum and calling it by that name, after the manner of the rulers of this world; nor of his striking his thigh with his hand and beating the tribunal with his feet; nor of his censuring and insulting those who did not applaud him nor shake their handkerchiefs, as is done in the theatres, nor bawl out and leap about after the manner of his partisans, both male and female, who were such disorderly listeners to him, but chose to hear reverently and modestly as in the house of God; nor of his unseemly and violent attacks in the congregation upon the expounders of the Word who have already departed this life, and his magnifying of himself, not like a bishop, but like a sophist and juggler; nor of his putting a stop to the psalms sung in honor of our Lord Jesus Christ, as the recent compositions of recent men, and preparing women to sing psalms in honor of himself in the midst of the Church. In the great day of the Paschal festival, which choristers one might shudder to hear. And besides, he acted on those bishops and presbyters, who fawned upon him in the neighboring districts and cities, to advance the like opinions in their discourses to their people.

3. For we may say, to anticipate a little what we intend to write below, that he does not wish to acknowledge that the Son of God came down from heaven. And this is a statement which shall not be made to depend on simple assertion; for it is proved abundantly by those memoranda which we sent you, and not least by that passage in which he says that Jesus Christ is from below. And they who sing his praise and eulogize him

among the people, declare that their impious teacher has come down as an angel from heaven. And such utterances the haughty man does not check, but is present even when they are made. And the again there are these women—these adopted sisters, as the people of Antioch call them—who are kept by him and by the presbyters and deacons with him, whose incurable sins in this and other matters, though he is cognizant of them, and has convicted them, he connives at concealing, with the view of keeping the men subservient to himself, and preventing them, by fear for their own position, from daring to accuse him in the matter of his impious words and deeds. Besides this, he has made his followers rich, and for that he is loved and admired by those who set their hearts on these things. But why should we write of these things? For, beloved, we know that the bishop and all the clergy ought to be an example in all good works to the people. Nor are we ignorant of the fact that many have fallen away through introducing these women into their houses, while others have fallen under suspicion. So that, even although one should admit that he has been doing nothing disgraceful in this matter, yet he ought at least to have avoided the suspicion that springs out of such a course of conduct, lest perchance some might be offended, or find inducement to imitate him. For how, then, should anyone censure another, or warn him to beware of yielding to greater familiarity with a woman, lest perchance he might slip, as it is written: if, although he has dismissed one, he has still retained two with him, and these in the bloom of their youth, and of fair countenance; and if when he goes away he takes them with him; and all this, too, while he indulges in luxury and surfeiting?

4. And on account of these things all are groaning and lamenting with themselves; yet they have such a dread of his tyranny and power that they cannot venture on accusing him. And of these things, as we have said already, one might take account in the case of a man who held Catholic sentiments and belonged to our own number; but as to one who has betrayed the mystery (of the faith), and who swaggers with the abominable heresy of Artemas,—for why should we hesitate to disclose his father?—we consider it unnecessary to exact of him an account for these things.

5. *Then at the close of the epistle they add the following words:*—We have been compelled, therefore, to excommunicate this man, who thus opposes God Himself, and refuses submission, and to appoint in his place another bishop for the Church Catholic, and that, as we trust, by the providence of God—namely, the son of Demetrianus, a man of blessed memory, and one who presided over the same Church with distinction in former times, Domnus by name, a man endowed with all the noble qualities which become a bishop. And this fact we have communicated to you in order that ye may write him, and receive letters of communion from him. And that other may write to Artemas, if it please him; and those who think with Artemas may hold communion with him, if they are so minded.

II.—Fragments Apparently of the Same Epistle of the Synod of Antioch;
To Wit, of that Part of It Which It is Agreed that Eusebius Left Unnoticed.

He says, therefore, in the commentaries (they speak of Paul), that he maintains the dignity of wisdom.

And thereafter:

If, however, he had been united according to formation and generation, this is what befalls the man. *And again*: For that wisdom, as we believe, was not congenerate with humanity substantially, but qualitatively.

And thereafter:

In what respect, moreover, does he mean to allege that the formation of Christ is different and diverse from ours, when we hold that, in this one thing of prime consequence,

His constitution differs from ours, to wit, that what in us is the interior man, is in Him the Word.

And thereafter:

If he means to allege that Wisdom dwells in Him as in no other, this expresses indeed the same mode of inhabitation, though it makes it excel in respect of measure and multitude;

He being supposed to derive a superior knowledge from the Wisdom, say for example, twice as large as others, or any other number of times as large; or, again, it may be less than twice as large a knowledge as others have. This, however, the catholic and ecclesiastical canons disallow, and hold rather that other men indeed received of Wisdom as an inspiration from without, which, though with them, is distinct from them; but that Wisdom in verity came of itself substantially into His body by Mary.

And after other matters:

And they hold that there are not two Sons. But if Jesus Christ is the Son of God, and if Wisdom also is the

Son of God; and if the Wisdom is one thing and Jesus Christ another, there are two Sons.

And thereafter:

Moreover understand (Paul would say) the union with Wisdom in a different sense, namely as being one according to instruction and participation; but not as if it were formed according to the substance in the body.

And after other matters:

Neither was the God who bore the human body and had assumed it, without knowledge of human affections in the first instance; nor was the human body without knowledge, in the first instance, of divine operations in him in whom He (the God) was, and by whom He wrought these operations. He was formed, in the first instance, as man in the womb; and, in the second instance, the God also was in the womb, united essentially with the human, that is to say, His substance being wedded with the man.

III.—From the Acts of the Disputation Conducted by Malchion Against Paul of Samosata.

The compound is surely made up of the simple elements, even as in the instance of Jesus Christ, who was made one (person), constituted by God the Word, and a human body which is of the seed of David, and who subsists without having any manner of division between the two, but in unity. You, however, appear to me to decline to admit a constitution after this fashion: to the effect that there is not in this person, the Son of God according to substance, but only the Wisdom according to participation. For you made this assertion, that the Wisdom bears dispensing, and therefore cannot be compounded; and you do not consider that the divine Wisdom remained undiminished, even as it was before it evacuated itself; and thus in this self-evacuation, which it took upon itself in compassion (for us), it continued undiminished and unchangeable. And this assertion you also make, that the Wisdom dwelt in Him, just as we also dwell in houses, the one in the other, and yet not as if we formed a part of the house, or the house a part of us.

IV.—A Point in the Same Disputation.

Did I not say before that you do not admit that the only-begotten Son, who is from all eternity before every creature, was made substantially existent in the whole person of the Savior; that is to say, was united *with Him* according to substance?

Elucidations.

I.
(The epistle written by Malchion, p. 169.)
Malchion, though a presbyter of Antioch, reflects the teaching of Alexandria, and illustrates its far-reaching influence. Firmilian, presiding at the Council of Antioch, was a pupil of Origen; and Dionysius was felt in the council, though unable to be present. Malchion and Firmilian, therefore, vindicate the real mind of Origen, though speaking in language matured and guarded. This council was, providentially, a rehearsal for Nicæa.

II.
(Putting a stop to psalms, etc., p. 170.)
Coleridge notes this, with an amusing comment on *Paulus Samosatenus*, and refers to Pliny's letter, of which

see vol. v. p. 604, this series. Jeremy Taylor, from whom Coleridge quotes, gives the passage of our author as follows: "Psalmos et cantus qui ad Dom. nostri J. C. honorem decantari solent, tanquam recentiores et a viris recentioris memoriæ editos, exploserit" (*Works*, ii. p. 281, ed. Bohn, 1844). Observe what Coleridge says elsewhere on errors attributed to Origen: "Never was a great man so misunderstood as Origen." He adds: "The *caro noumenon* was what Origen meant by Christ's 'flesh consubstantial with His Godhead.'"

Find this and other great works of the early Church Fathers at lighthousechristianpublishing.com.

Our Father who art in heaven, hallowed be thy name.
Thy kingdom come, Thy will be done, on earth as it is in heaven.
Give us this day our daily bread and forgive us our trespasses as we forgive those who trespass against us.
And lead us not into temptation, but deliver us from evil, for Thine is the kingdom, the power and the glory. Forever and ever.

Amen

Hail Mary full of grace, the Lord is with thee. Blessed art thou amongst women and blessed is the fruit of thy womb Jesus. Holy Mary mother of God, pray for us sinners, now and the hour of our death.

www.ingramcontent.com/pod-product-compliance
Lightning Source LLC
Chambersburg PA
CBHW052205070526
44585CB00017B/2077